Pacific Verses

ANDRÉ BLONDEL TONLEU MENDOU

Pacific Verses

Poetry

ISBN
Hardcover: 978-1-965134-63-4
Paperback: 978-1-965134-64-1

Prologue

A frequent question my interlocutors often ask is: what does an ambassador do?

I have no intention of listing the duties of a diplomatic agent here, but certainly, an ambassador writes and listens to many speeches. Some aim to change the course of political affairs, others are demonstrations of skill, or more precisely, "speaking skill," while others are mere ceremonial or customary speeches to fill an event.

The ultimate goal of a speech is to convey a message using the beauty and power of words. This is exactly what André Blondel Tonleu Mendou does in "Versets du Pacifique," but through the art of poetry.

Le Pacifique evokes an ideal. It sometimes suggests something exotic, inviting daydreams, utopias. It is the unattainable—or rather the unattained—which contrasts with our current context as well as our experience during the pandemic. A word with countless meanings, just as the author, a certified and award-winning master of eloquence, possesses many talents.

Can one be a citizen and a committed poet in 2022? He shows us that it is possible.

"Versets du Pacifique" confirms André Blondel's spectacular ability to juggle words, both written and spoken, while giving them deep meaning. As the pages unfold, the reader is immersed in reflection. There is no room for emptiness but only for hope and the expression of wishes.

For example, the desire to see the african continent finally emancipated from the frustration of imitating the West (lowercase intentional), which has sought and continues to seek to impose itself as a model. The abused and disillusioned Africa should, on the contrary, deserve the reverence owed to a mother, the cradle of all humanity. Blondel calls for the self-determination and affirmation of Africans, as well as respect for their autonomy. He confronts us with our demons in his invectives against discrimination, post-colonial stereotypes, and imperialist fantasies that still sometimes persist and lead us to reflect on our behaviors, including those that are unconscious, whether we are actors, witnesses, or victims of these unhealthy processes.

For the author, politics should be a near-priestly commitment, but the game of political parties and corruption too often prevents the building of healthy and effective institutions ("République bananière" and "Opposant tropical").

Through his poetics, we are invited to introspection as well as to an analysis of the world around us. The author wisely encourages us to change this world, pointing out inequalities. Poetry thus becomes a tool against isolation, self-centeredness, and, above all, Western-centric thinking. It appears as a remedy to break down barriers, to tear down the walls that need to be demolished.

Aimé Césaire said, 'Poetry is an insurrection against society': here, Blondel's poignant plea invites us to revolt against this society of solitude, against hatred, against divisions. Through his verses, he speaks of human rights, particularly those of albinos, refugees, youth, and women, whom he considers "queens (...) born to illuminate the world" but who still remain "toys of history." The author defines xenophobia as a "childhood illness," an illness that, ironically, only seems to affect adults. Who is the Black Man if not my brother? Blondel's decisive activism in his career seeps through the lines, striking straight to the heart. It is no coincidence that we met at a conference against hate speech. Fraternity is indeed embedded in almost every text in "Versets du Pacifique." It became evident to many during the COVID-19 pandemic, at least to those who recognized it; sometimes, it is our shared human vulnerabilities that bring us closer. Citizens and political leaders have lessons to learn from the cataclysm that the health crisis represented. As the text "Grasping the Bull by the Horns" reminds us, the pandemic highlighted all the inequalities that define our societies, both in the North and the South, without distinction. People have changed with this experience or must hurry to do so, and politics must change too: everyone now understands that it is only united that we can face crises.

Beyond the great inspirations on global issues, André Blondel also touches the most sensitive and profound chords of our soul by speaking to us of feelings and relationships, in one word: Love. Let the reader not see a contradiction here; quite the contrary. Jacques Prévert himself defined poetry as "the loveliest nickname one gives to life," and love or friendship is fortunately a part of it. And what better medium than poetry to express it? Verse after verse, the poet becomes intimate through a confession that invites us to look at ourselves in the mirror, deep into our hearts. Blondel unites Love for a dear one with love for noble causes, which coexist in righteous men, those destined to make a difference in this world.

Pierre Bourdieu, during a debate at the University Palace of Strasbourg, said: "If there's a group we could turn to for role models, it would be the poets! (…) They are people without a market who have so much investment, so much belief in what they do (…).” In donning his poetic garb, André Blondel calls for the realization of an ideal, his ideal: to pacify the world, make it better, with a place for everyone and respect for all.

"All men are born free and equal in rights": *"Versets du Pacifique"* reminds us of this in the most melodious and eloquent way. We must hear this cry of hope and embrace this ode to unity, respecting and celebrating the diversities that enrich us, for, as recited in "Djihad," it is the colors that make a carpet beautiful. Let us rebuild a lost paradise where all can live in peace.

Enjoy your reading.

Her Excellency Sylvie Bollini
Ambassador of the Republic of San Marino

Foreword

This poetic work attempts to offer some ethical, even peaceful, guidelines for a new world. It was born from an observation: globalization and democratization have awakened nationalisms, identity aspirations, and ethnic conflicts around the world. Since the end of the Cold War, struggles for self-recognition and group identity have become the main paradigms of political conflicts. Many conflicts involve not only states, either directly or through armed groups or rebels but also, within certain states, linguistic and cultural communities fighting in the name of their identities. Paradoxically, the thaw in international relations, exacerbated by a new form of neocolonialism, has left people in a state of impoverishment beyond reality. This is why, in Africa, people struggling to survive must forge a new path to resist the human condition. The ethnic-regional powder kegs in Africa, overturning the values table; the feeling of marginalization of certain ethnic groups; economic conflicts over access to land and natural resources, including water and forests, have led to political-administrative adjustments, carving out political regulation on precarious balances. Ethnic and identity overheating has been used either as an excuse for redrawing electoral boundaries or as a pretext, presented as saviors of peace and national unity.

The protection of human rights has not escaped this awakening of difference and the perception of the other as much as the representation of oneself. Many conflicts have their belligerent foundations in the feeling of exclusion and domination of public affairs by a sociologically determined group. These conflicts have been the cause of serious and massive human rights violations. Societies that are partisan and scarred emerge from these ethnic-identitarian whirlpools, constituting a serious handicap to the construction of a rule-of-law society.

Yet, from this disarray, a plea gradually emerges, showing that one does not so easily rid oneself of the *"lost paradise."* As if this were not enough, the latest mistake of our current global civilization is the vandalism of development. What we call development in the world today has been a vast myth and an ideology that has justified the irresponsible lifestyle we suffer from today. It was presented to us in Africa as a project of progress for the people, "a glimmer of hope." Development has become our drama, a machine for producing inequalities and misery, indebtedness and exclusion, despair and precariousness. But in protecting essentially hegemonic colonial interests, *"the goat browses where it is tied."*

What happened for the dream to turn into a nightmare? We have simply forgotten that humanity has spiritual foundations, and any process that destroys these foundations will eventually lead to a catastrophe. It is the imperial mode beyond the African dream.

As Edgar Morin insightfully observed, development as it is experienced today "ignores what is neither calculable nor measurable, that is, life, suffering, joy, love, and its only measure of satisfaction is in growth" (of the Production, productivity, monetary income). Conceived solely in quantitative terms, it ignores qualities: the qualities of existence, the qualities of solidarity, the qualities of the environment, the qualities of life, human riches that are non-calculable and non-monetizable; it ignores the gift, marginalization, honor, and conscience. Its approach sweeps away the cultural treasures and knowledge of archaic and traditional civilizations: the blind and crude concept of underdevelopment disintegrates the arts of living and the wisdom of millennia-old cultures."[1]

We are faced with fierce vandalism that produces genuine moral and psychological underdevelopment. African states beat to the rhythm of "Républiques bananières," covered by a painkiller called the planetary village, leading to a situation fraught with the threat of annihilation.

All the sages of our planet continue to warn us about the current lifestyle that has deified money. The world's greats remain deaf to these warnings. We will pay for this deafness sooner or later. It is impossible to aggress nature to the point of wanting to destroy it without it eventually reacting.

We Africans cannot continue to passively and helplessly watch the expansion of the civilization of development in its current harmfulness. The time has come to think of other ways of life and other ways of being based on the quality of existence. *Versets du Pacifique* comes at a crucial moment, challenging racism, discrimination against black people, apple of discord, chauvinism, racial supremacy, police violence, and acculturation to make Africans understand that they are also humans beyond the freedom-restraining virus that

---

[1]Edgar Morin, "Pour une politique de l'humanité," Le Monde, August 26, 2002.

has protected imperial power to establish the law of the lions in Africa, plunging them into the dark night; the spirit of good in secularism, linked to the great wisdom of our cultural traditions, offers today sources of inspiration for another horizon, one that guarantees the human being a pleasant and humane physical and social environment. That is why the author of this poetic work revisits the fundamentals of African communitarianism: "ubuntu," which embodies love for others that extends beyond immediate proximity to the distant, hospitality, and brotherhood. Well-being comes at this price in choosing a life attuned to the high wisdom of Christ: what does it profit a man to gain the universe if he loses his soul, if he annihilates his own life, if he destroys all his future chances?

Moreover, the waywardness of our society, if not the current world, can be termed egomania or the idolatry of an oversized and absolutized "self." This neologism of egomania refers to the consequence of a reality mentioned in the Book of Genesis when the serpent tells Adam and Eve that they will be like God. Today, this demonic prophecy has been fulfilled, and we have created a civilization with the pretense of being God itself in all its powers, resulting in an ego that inflates to the extreme. Man has begun to live from vanity, aggressiveness, and a desire for domination because he no longer recognizes his limits. He climbs ever higher with a ladder eaten by termites. Yet he says to himself, "I am capable of going higher." His vanity leads him to worship his own navel. Determined by this spirit, each person seeks to become the center of the world and is confronted with other "egos" as inflated with vanity as their own. Peoples fall into this game of self-deification.

The fierce struggle then becomes the concrete modality of human relations, overshadowing the primordial truth of cooperation and solidarity. There is intense competition in creating everything that destroys humanity. One must surpass others in their capacity for harm and destruction; this is how respect is earned. This quest for the "superego" has become an obsession for both individuals and states, some of which do not hesitate to call themselves superpowers. Even tribes deify themselves, as seen in societies like Rwanda, leading to genocides. Entire regions are engulfed in flames. Terrorism becomes institutionalized, and some nations are labeled as "Rogue states" and classified as "axis of evil."

Today, the task is to rediscover the modesty and fragility of our human condition and to relearn solidarity in order to live and survive together. Jesus designated this requirement with the term love, a word that nations do not understand and yet must be integrated into their vocabulary and socio-economic-political practices if humanity is to have a future.

However, through this apparent diversity, I believe there exists a true unity. The reader will indeed discover that several key ideas are illustrated through the verses:

–The human being is a radically limited entity, or to use more philosophical terms, man is fundamentally marked by finitude. True liberation can only be that which acknowledges this radical finitude. This means that the path to freedom is always a path where one learns to recognize that one is not all-powerful in constructiveness or destructiveness.

–Limited by sometimes considerable conditioning (somatic, psychic, social), man always retains a zone of freedom that allows him to believe in humanity. There is no true freedom except that which fully considers reality in all its ambiguity, even its contradictions.

–Moral, even pacific, action is always a regulator of conflicts of value. To humanize oneself is to reject the double purism of either/or all-at-once; it is, definitively, to seek one's humanity in the compromises of always imperfect decisions and in the slowness of time. That is why humanity and patience are at the heart of all moral life.

–Every human being, no matter how troubled or sinful, is called to holiness. This may be one of the most central affirmations of *Versets du Pacifique.* No one is condemned to remain eternally in failure or simply in hibernation. May these pages help the reader to increasingly embrace the cry of this multidimensional human who dreams of the African as *"A being in his own right and not a being entirely apart."*

This document does not claim to offer a total and all-encompassing view of the realities studied. The author's modest means could scarcely support such a claim. Nevertheless, the analytical tools proposed can now serve to expand the scope of the debate, as this is an initial field that has been crossed.

Dr. Jean YEMENE KENNE
Cameroon, May 20, 2022

Dedication

To Anatole and Sabine Mendou—my parents and first fans;

And to Hadrien Elie and Noémie Sabine, whose bright rays

Make the world a more wonderful place!

Contents

Ubuntu[2]

The diversity of colors in a carpet adds to its beauty,
It should foster the peace of entities,
Which do not always harmonize their golden colors!

The African is a being in his own right,
And not a being entirely apart!
Focusing on differences is a part
Of social tensions, and Mother Africa
Must celebrate in joy
Her various accents!

Otherwise, she will always be dragging the devil
By the tail and Africans,
Becoming wolves to other Africans.

Ubuntu is about helping one's brothers,
Because they are our brothers,
It is believing that we exist
Because our brothers exist!

It is not about hating your brother,
Or pretending to love your brother,
It is about helping your brother in brotherhood,
Working with your brother in hospitality!

It is teaching him to fish for fish;
And to hunt for hedgehogs;

---

[2] Thoughts Following Xenophobic Acts in South Africa or African Conflicts with Other Africans, Resulting from Jealousy in the African Diaspora Community Where Clans Clash, and the Tribalism that Strongly Affects National Communities!

It is showing solidarity;
Among sisters, among brothers!

Embezzling public funds is not Ubuntu!
Misappropriating businesses is not Ubuntu!
Sacrificing the future of your country for personal
interests is not Ubuntu!

Where is this glorified Africa?
And its values of Honesty!
Where is this Africa of solidarity?
And its consolidated communities!
Where is this Africa,
Master of magnified values?

Xenophobia is a childhood disease,
That undermines the fertile friendliness,
Of communities already not very versatile!
It will divert Africa from its coveted destiny,
And from its past, built on the heights of dignity!

To be a brother is to be able to travel from Cape to
Cairo,
To be a brother is to embody all of Africa,
To be a brother is to celebrate our diverse accents,
To be a brother is to show fraternity,
To be a brother is to be completely sincere,
As our smile is among the clearest,
As we oppose communal hatred,
With love for the neighbor, love for the brother!

We are all humans!
We all come from a human family,
We all come from a village in Africa,

We are all children of Africa,
We are the children of one mother,
That mother at the center of oceans and seas!

Africa is our motherland,
Africa is our brotherhood!
Africa is unique and chivalrous,
Africa must remain hospitable!

Because alone, one might go fast,
But together we will certainly go further!

Umuntu ngumuntu ngabantu![3]

---

[3] African Proverb which means People are people.

Men Entirely Apart[4]

Today, the spirit of racism;
Still lurks on the horizon;
Today, the spirit of racism
Still hovers in the air of our era!

Even today, the Black man;
Remains a victim of discrimination;
And the greatest segregation.
He still endures humiliations;
In a world that should be
Adorned with the greatest civilizations!

The law has always been harsher
When one is Black!
The Black man,
Still suffers in body
And soul from simply being Black!

The Black man
Remains a sub-human,
A man entirely apart;
And not apart in full,
Simply because he is Black!

Discrimination remains subtle, like
A hand of iron in a velvet glove.
He survives like a chameleon that changes color,
He resists like a wolf with a flavor,
A scent of sacrificed lamb!

---

[4] In tribute to George Floyd, cowardly murdered by the American police, and to the defenders of social justice

Segregation remains institutionalized and
systematized,
It remains subtle and systemic;
And to some extent, epidemic.

The Black man faces a system
Greased and established, which, like a real problem,
And like a pebble in his shoes,
Blocks his integration into the system!

The Black man still lives in an islet
Of misery at the heart of a vast ocean of wealth;
He remains condemned to ghettos
Miserable and oscillating between sinful opulence,
Cleared by the majority adorned with duchess.
He remains condemned to a certain smallness!
Yet we are all humans!
Yet we all belong to the human race!

If an African is hurt, the blood that will flow will be
red!
If an Indian is hurt, the blood that will flow will be
red!
If a Caucasian is hurt, the blood that will flow will be
red!

No matter our skin color,
We are all humans!
We are all born free and equal!

The color of the skin,
The color of the eyes,
Or the texture of the hair,

Do not determine the wish
To be happy or unhappy!

Human dignity alone
Grants such value!
This dignity is a right,
Simply by virtue of being human!
This dignity is not a choice!

It is a right!
A right of humans!
Because they are humans!

Why so much hatred!
Why so much pain!

We have the historical responsibility
To break these barriers!
We have the political responsibility
To advocate for and respect
The dignity of every human being!

Regardless of ethnicity,
Regardless of heritage,
Regardless of nationality!

We have the historical responsibility
To make the world a peaceful place,
Fostering philanthropic values,
And opposing misanthropic tendencies!

Even if they did not give us

Love,
Let us give them the love they
Did not give us!

We belong to a new generation,
We have known neither slavery nor colonization,
We must make the world a sunny place,
Of social justice, racial justice, freedom, and equality!

No to racism;
It is a shame for humanity!
No to chauvinism;
It is a disease for interculturality!

No to racial supremacy;
It is a cancer that undermines society!
No to police violence;
It is the agent of brutality!
However, let us not be afraid to denounce!
Let us never be afraid to denounce!
Let us not be afraid to resist!

Denounce every racist act!
Denounce every segregationist act!
Denounce every tribalist act!

Resist every racist ideology,
Resist every chauvinistic act!
Resist every clannish tendency!
Let us not be afraid!
Do not be afraid!
Let us never be afraid!

Let us believe in social justice!
Let us believe in social fairness!
Let us believe in social equality!
Let us believe in social equity!
Let us not be afraid!
Do not be afraid!
Let us believe in the strength of the law!
And not in the law of force!
Let us believe in the power of just laws!
And not in the power of unjust laws!
For an unjust law,
No one is obligated to obey![5]
No justice, no peace!
No justice, no peace!

---

[5] Saint Augustine

Lost Paradise[6]

In Africa, they mock his language;
He speaks other languages;
He dreams of living beyond the Mediterranean;
He dreams of a paradisiacal life beyond the Pyrenees!
In Africa, he imitates the West;
He thinks like Westerners;
He acts like Westerners;
He eats like Westerners;
He dresses like Westerners;
Forgets that he is still on the continent!
In Africa, he dreams of a distant paradise;
A Paradise set in a land of glory;
A promised land where water flows like a torrent;
A land where milk and honey flow;
A paradise where the abundance of salt
Is like the stars in the sky!

In Africa, he speaks French, English;
Speaks Spanish, Portuguese;
Speaks Italian, Mandarin, Japanese;
Speaks Russian, German, or Dutch;
He is the best student among the Cantonese!

In the West, he believes he is European, but
Faces victimization.
He calls himself American, but
Faces discrimination!

Condemned to generational exile,
He lives in cultural ghettoization;

---

[6] For Those Uprooted from Their Native Land.

Forced to make efforts
Mechanical rather than strong,
Forced to make efforts
Like those demanded of oxen,
Buffaloes, or donkeys!

In the West, his life is stalled;
And remains as fragile as an egg!

He immediately dreams of the lost paradise,
Facing a life that has become harsh.
He remains nostalgic for a past,
A past that doesn't seem to have passed;
A past he no longer wants to abandon;
Because he is confronted with the sad reality!

Today, an eternal student,
He remains nostalgic for his privileges,
Traditional, his titles of nobility;
Like a bird, he sees his honor
Flying away on the trees;
His dream country seems to be a nightmare;
And his dream life, a real racket!

He becomes a defender of his ancestral culture,
Positioning himself as a masterful unifier;
And a promoter of liberal values!

He feels invested with a presidential mission,
Because he believes he has enough wings,
He returns to the mother tongues,
To limit the impact of the cultural genocide,
Which threatens the people of his nation,
But especially those of his generation!

He begins to dress like in his country;
He learns the values and customs of his land;
He mentions at every opportunity his glorious past;
The glorious past of his people, their fortunate empires!
He is the African immigrant; he is the African man!
He lives like a Westerner in Africa;
And lives like an African in the West;
He is not African in Africa;
But becomes so when he leaves Africa;
He is not Western in the West;
But becomes so when he leaves the West!
How will Africa be respected?
If we do not show authenticity!
How will the African be glorified?
If he remains a beggar sitting on an under-exploited diamond mine!
If it is true that a fish out of water
Cannot live in muddy water,
So is the case of the African who, outside his cultural network,
Outside his natural environment of hope,
Remains a mere plaything of history!

More than ever, the African must be proud!
Proud of his Africanness,
Proud of his identity!
Proud, simply Proud!
More than ever, the African must know that he is a son of Africa,
Before conquering this tragic-comic world!

He must know that, although the bird may fly in the sky,
The night will always remind it that it has a nest![7]

That his culture is to him what water is to nature.
When nature lacks water, it dries up and dies.
And that, deprived of his culture, he is a dead man!

That counting day and night the fortune of the neighbor
Does not make us an authentic person.
That one can only be proud of oneself by the fragrance
Of one's own culture!

The African must love his country!
He must love Africa and its beautiful landscapes!
He must revere this sacred land, a source of life!
Only under this condition could he discover his paradise:

Africa and its lands with a taste of honey!
Africa and its rays of sunshine!
Africa and its iconic sites!
Africa and its authentic dances!
Africa and its peaceful people!
Africa and its magical wisdoms!

---

[7] African Wisdom

Transatlantic Love[8]

The binguiste was back in his homeland;[9]
After years in France, he was back,
A grand return with a carnival flair,
He was back on a white horse by day,
And in a setting worthy of grand festivals!

He came to court his singular sweetheart,
This unknown woman, with a knightly gaze,
Whom he loved without knowing,
And who loved him without necessarily knowing!

His family received numerous applications,
He had to choose one application,
A choice that would highlight the candidate's
Physical, intellectual, and cultural assets!

At the scent of Barbara's candidacy,
The knight, struck by a lightning bolt, did not hesitate
To let himself be carried away by this beauty,
A beauty punctuated by a killer gaze,
A beauty with a statue-like stare,
A gaze that strikes like a lightning bolt!

Shaped like a guitar, with her generous curves,
The Western knight was instantly happy,
He was, as if by magic, in love!

---

[8] Verses for Expatriates Returning to Their Homeland in Search of Love!

[9] Refers to immigrants living in Europe or the Americas who return to their homeland to find their soulmate.

The wedding was beautiful, with a carnival flair,
The wedding was majestic and even pompous,
Love made it seem like a fusion of lovers,
The wedding was joyful and convivial!

The two families felt blessed by the gods,
And went to the airport,
An airport, a bird's flight from the port,
To send off the lovebirds,
Who were to soar into the skies,
For a honeymoon with languorous accents!

A Honeymoon Among Exotic Flowers,
A Honeymoon with the Taste of Honey,
A Honeymoon as Beautiful as the Rooster,
And its Gleaming Feathers,
A Honeymoon with the Scents and Colors of Love,
The Love that was Theirs!

The Love that Made Them Dream of Each Other,
The Love that Drew Them to One Another,
Like the Fragrance of Flowers Draws Bees,
Like the Rooster Seduces the Hen with Its Beautiful
Plumage!

In Paris, Barbara, as if struck by lightning,
And like a chameleon changes its face,
She completely changes her image!
She changes color in the midst of winter,
And turns her winter coat inside out!

The knight no longer recognized his astral flower,
Now given over to mercenary gallantry.
She no longer fulfilled her marital obligations,

Nor her family duties!

Because too beautiful to take them on,
Because too emancipated to take them on,
Because she had become a bit too feminist,
Because she had become a bit too materialistic,
Because she had become a bit too corporate!

One certain morning, the hated police
Arrested her, like a sacrificial lamb,
Based on a complaint filed
By her beloved, by her sweetheart!

In the depths and abysses
Of his dark cell,
He realized he was in ruins!

Condemned to face a criminal record,
That would weigh upon his shoulders like a sword,
The eternal sword of Damocles,

Condemned for having loved a woman,
A woman from his own country,
A woman of his own country,
In accordance with the pious wishes of the people of
his country!

Condemned to bear the shame of his family,
Condemned for having loved a girl,
And for simply loving a girl,
Beyond the Atlantic!

Love imprisons,

And if loving is a crime?
Must one, then, plead guilty?

He regretted seeking
A love that remained perched,
In the trees of sacred forests
And the shrubs of haunted savannas!

He regretted those Parisian lovers
Who flirted with him,
Declaring their flame!
The flame that burned within them,
For a knight who, to these beauties,
Remained the eternal darling!

At that particular moment when
The Atlantic wind had carried away
His emotions, his loving sensations,
To distant islands, to faraway lands!

In the evening of long heartbeats,
He quietly understood in his heart,
That love knows no borders,
That love is without borders,
That transatlantic love was risky!

That this new kind of love
Would be like that rare fish which, once caught,
Without committing the slightest sin,
Slips delicately back into the ocean,
And offers itself without hesitation to the predator,
From the very first hour!

The Sacrifice of Love

By dedicating his life to love,
Because he made it triumph,
Contrary to the wishes of Emperor
Claudius II, who feared that love might
Hinder the military commitment of lovers,

Valentine, that great defender of marriage
And of love within marriage,
Could not imagine without hesitation;
That such a battle, sacred with glamour,
Would be experienced today with so much humor!

Entrepreneurs becoming more in love,
Because Valentine's Day brings them joy,
With businesses boasting prestigious revenues,
Driven by a day dedicated to lovers!

Love becoming much more passionate,
And lovebirds much less rational,
Gazing into each other's eyes,
With their sights sometimes fixed on the skies,
But forgetting to look towards the same bridges!

In the name of the celebration of love,
Couples have come to hate each other,
In the name of the celebration of love,
Families have fallen apart,
In the name of the celebration of love,
Some gazes have met,
But alas! others have drifted away!

Does the celebration of love truly reflect love?

Is offering a rose on this day enough,
To claim love for all eternity?
What will happen on the other days?

Love is vital to humanity,
And cannot be limited to a festivity,
That takes place on a famous day in February,
For its flame remains lit for eternity!

To be in love is to cherish one's sweetheart,
To love one's beloved
With great civility,
And eternal magnanimity!

It's about sharing good cheer,
Letting your heart speak,
Even in deep resentment!

But to be in love is also,
To love social justice,
To love social progress,
To love social well-being!

Being in love is not just about,
Gazing into each other's eyes,
Or soaring into the skies!

It's also about loving noble causes,
Embracing noble values,
And ultimately, it's knowing that time is never
wasted,
When you take all the time you need,
For the triumph of noble causes!

Causes that also strengthen love,
From dawn to dusk,
Causes that uplift love,
Causes that sanctify love,
And not just for a moment;
But for all time!

For the great joy of communities,
For the great joy of societies!
For the great joy of sweethearts!
For the great joy of beloveds!

Valentine is dead,
May love be strong!

They Are Human Too[10]

Albinism is not a crime,
An albino is not a criminal,
It's a genetic condition,
A simple deficiency of melanin!

They have rights like every human being;
They are fully human!

We live in a world that hunts and pursues them,
We live in a world that massively despises them!

In Tanzania, they are still sacrificed,
For mystical rites and rituals;
In Tanzania, they are a source of magical power.
In Malawi, the albino is hunted and sacrificed,
To ensure the economic prosperity of some,
To satisfy the "power-hungry" appetites of others.
In Malawi, the albino remains a subhuman!

Despite his sense of humor,
He rarely finds love.
Despite his right to life and survival,
He risks being sacrificed upon his arrival in life,
At the altar of mystical and metaphysical practices!

The albino child still divides couples,
The albino child is still a mystic who
Portends no smooth tomorrows!

---

[10] For the recognition of the rights of albino individuals!

Will there come a day when their right to life will be
upheld,
Will there come a day when their right to health will
be strengthened,
Will there come a day when their right to safety will
be a reality,
Will there come a day when their right to dignity will
be respected!

Unfortunately, that day has not yet arrived!
Unfortunately, that day still seems far off!

When will that day come?
When? When will that day come?
In 100 years? In 50 years?

The tears and the extent of violations in these times
Demand that it be now or never!

Simple passivity is synonymous with complicity,
In this sacred fight aimed at restoring the dignity
Of a minority, oh so marginalized,
For years!

Education on albinism would be one key to
resolution!
Raising awareness of rights and the law would be
another key solution!
State repression of offenders would be an evolution
In this struggle against discrimination,
This struggle against stigmatization!

Because albinos must be protected!
Because albinos must be secured!
Because albinos are born to shine!

Grabbing the Bull by the Horns

2020 will forever mark the pages of history!
Yet, not long ago,
We were at the beginning of this story,
Which, like the morning sun adorned
With its shimmering and vibrant colors,
Gave us real reasons
To always keep hope alive!

Hope for a beautiful ending to the story;
The hope of smiling at the end
Of this story!

That magical moment had shone,
Like a great beacon of the night,
A bright light of hope,
Which numbs all thoughts of despair!

2020 has thus already found its place in the annals of
history;
And yet, we cannot forget that it was a year
Full of twists and countless detours on the
scoreboard,
A year of emotions and renowned compassion,

A year marked and paced by a loathed living being,
A tiny creature, visible only through a microscope!

The world was shaken, dreams crumbled,
Planes grounded, countries confined,
The economy on life support, and even anesthetized,
In a social climate that, far from rosy,

Turned out to be mostly gloomy!

In this climate of a health war,
We washed our hands.
Many times, we washed our hands,
And we continue to wash our hands,
To avoid the spread of a virus
That never stops ruling;
That never stops imposing its law!

The act of handwashing reminds us
Of a certain unethical Pontius Pilate,
Who, through such symbolism,
Dismissed a political cause,
When he could have made a historic decision,
To change the course of the legal world,
And fully assume such a decision!

Should we then wash our hands?
Should we wash our hands of this difficult year?
Should we then wash our hands
Every time the winds blow against us?
Every time the world turns against us?
Should we remain citizens who wash their hands,
Because they cannot make a historic decision?

Let us not definitively wash our hands when
The world faces the gravest injustices!
When societies normalize inequality,
While discarding the norm!

Let us not wash our hands:
When we face situations,
That seem beyond our control,

When we can, through our efforts,
Shake the trees to improve
The course of our societies and our own reality!

Let us be the actors of our own story!
And never hesitate to grab the bull by the horns,
To influence history and own our decisions!
Let us never give up!
Let us not lower our hands,
Let us be the actors shaping the world; let us make
history!
If we do not want to be subject to history!

No matter the mysteries
That the coming years may hold for us,
There is at least one reality we can control:
Hope in every ambiguous situation,
And hard work in the face of difficulties!

Let us never stop dreaming,
Let us never stop hoping,
No matter the contradictions of life!
No matter the various circumstances,
Or the various conjectures of life!

Let us never forget that success does not
Always come overnight,
And that a child who wants to learn to eat
The feast of the grown-ups often bites their tongue,
Because it is through perseverance
That one always ends up rising, always prospering!

Let us never forget that life is like a rainbow,

And sometimes it takes rain or sunshine
To discover its great splendor and its radiant colors!

Let us finally recognize that because
We are the actors of our own story,
Soon, the sun will extend its spectrum,
It will return, shining among the stars;
Then, in every grave, the extinguished ashes will awaken,
Everywhere, the flames of life will burn once again!

After the Night, the Dawn

The world has been shaken
By an underestimated pandemic;
A pandemic that this year,
Will revolutionize mindsets!

Nothing will ever be the same,
The world must look ahead!

Politics will no longer be the same,
Political parties will be less partisan,
Political consensus will take the lead,
Against party discipline and partisanship
That stands in the way of any emerging crisis
management!

A health crisis calls for the sacred union
Of all to defeat a hated enemy!

Hospitals have become overwhelmed
And it is urgent to relieve them.
The outdated healthcare system
Needs to be re-adapted;
Re-adapted for societies
That evolve with realities
Often overlooked in terms of health!

The pandemic heralds the golden age
Of remote work as a treasure;
For a multitude of employers,
A multitude of unions
For whom pandemic telework
Must become endemic!

Because it brings happiness
In times of misfortune,
Because it allows life to be lived,
And fosters the instinct for survival,
Remote work, far from being dormant,
Should become permanent,
For the employers who want it,
For the workers who want it!

The pandemic brings back to light,
Human rights that are out of date!
The right to an internet connection;
Which guarantees existence in a world,
Marked by virtual education
And the rise of artificial intelligence!

Must fully embrace
The realities of a technological world
To craft scientific recipes
That, like a wave of a magic wand,
Will change this post-pandemic world!

The pandemic restores air quality,
By rekindling the taste for the outdoors.
Species have diversified,
And the environment has regenerated!

Environmental protection remains possible,
Whether through policy-making,
Or in economically-driven projects:
Promoting the environment is not impossible!

At the twilight of such a tragic pandemic,

We should no longer see the glass as half empty;
But see it as half full!

It is time to seek that glimmer of hope,
That heralds optimistic tomorrows,
It is not the time to sink into despair
And remain condemned to the days ahead,
Oh, how they are dressed in worry, with pessimistic
hues!

After the long pandemic night,
The dawn will come!

Imperial World[11]

They call certain languages
Patois or dialect,
Because they supposedly lack clear language,
And form sub-languages,
Compared to their "true" languages!

They are expatriates in other countries,
Yet others become immigrants
When they arrive in their land!

They are national heroes when they
Show resistance even by chance;
Yet elsewhere, resistors are maquisards,
Troublemakers in troubled waters without real hope!

They ask us to protect our leopards,
Our monkeys, our tigers, and jaguars,
They ask us to protect our lions and cheetahs,
Our baobabs, tamarind trees, and water lilies,
Yet they are the greatest polluters!

The future of southern peoples
Doesn't seem to concern the North,
Which always presents to nations
A miserable vision of the African,
A pitiful vision of the South American,
As an eternal beggar
Sitting on a mine of gold or diamonds!

When we know that there is also an Africa

---

[11] For a more equitable world!

That is emerging, an Africa that makes the pride
Of its sons and daughters, just like the
Eiffel Tower in Paris, the CN Tower in Toronto,
Or the monuments of Saint John,
Madrid, Lisbon, or Washington!
When we know that Africa is the cradle
Of nations, the cradle of civilizations!

Because for them, Africa remains a hell
On which a category of individuals dwells,
Because for them, Africa remains wild,
Because for them, domestic and companion animals
Are lions and leopards,
In an Africa on the margins of the world of
Civilization.

An Africa of Tarzan,
Where people still live by hunting and gathering,
Where people still dress in animal skins
And the leaves of tall trees!
Because for them, Africa is a zoo,
A zoo evolving in troubled waters,
Reminding them of Man in a state of nature!

Because for them, Africa remains rural,
Because for them, it can never be bourgeois!

Their national law is international,
Their values are international,
Their opinion is international,
Their language is transnational!

The international community
Remains a clan of a few nations,

Turning International Law
Into a true Imperial Law!

The Rights of African Nations,
Becoming international law,
And Western national law,
Imposing itself in international law!

The international community
Remains a ghost,
A cloudy and nebulous reality.
It is real on this side of the Pyrenees,
And virtual beyond!

It intervenes urgently when
Its interests are threatened,
And patiently when the stakes
Play into its hand!

Africa must take charge of its destiny,
It must write its own history,
A history that spans north and south of the Sahara,
A history of glory and dignity!
A history that reflects the version
Told by the lions, not by the hunters,
A history that glorifies them eternally,
In the tales and stories of the hunt!

It will prioritize African solutions
To African problems.
It should make culture a lever for
Pan-African growth.
It will adopt a uniform diplomacy,

An atypical defense,
A prolific economy!

It should make Africa the center of
The world's influence, a terrestrial Eldorado worthy
of its history,
Glorious and enviable!

It will no longer vegetate on the periphery of
globalization.
Africa, like that firefly in the heart of the night,
It, Africa, will illuminate the world with its bright
rays.

Law of Lions

The collapse of the Berlin Wall
Signals the end of an international game,
And its many stakes!

The bipolar world order
Suddenly becomes unipolar!
And in a work with a highly imaginative title,
Fukuyama proclaims the end of history,
Marked by an Americanization
Of the law of nations.
The Last Man would be American!

The world stands powerless,
Witnessing an Americanization of international law,
The collapse of the international game,
Through the hyperpower of an actor,
Who, by circumstance, becomes dominant!

The world stands powerless,
Watching the politicization of law,
And the juridification of politics,
Turning the strongest into the legal Jupiter,
Of a world without contracts, a world without law!

Yet, Law is nothing but a rule of the game,
Between the nations participating in the game.
However, for law to be called Law,
The game must exist,
And for the game to exist, there must be at least two!

Unfortunately, there is only one actor,
An actor who is the grand master of the stakes.

Therefore, there can be no game;
No more rules of the game,
And the disappearance of the Law of nations,
For the triumph of the law of lions!

We live under the empire of the law of the strongest,
A law that imposes itself on the weaker!

When there is no longer an international game,
There are no more international laws,
But essentially an imperial Law!

However, the history of nations teaches us,
That it is the wheel of history that reigns,
That the judgment of history is final,
That the judgment of history is most severe!

Should we then laugh at international law?
Or celebrate the funeral of such an imperial law?

The history of nations teaches us that
He who weaves his destiny with threads
Of betrayal and cowardice will pay a high price,
The penalty of the tribunal of history!
That the strongest is never strong enough,
To remain the grand master of the game,
If he does not submit to the force of law!

The history of nations teaches us that
Every empire must perish!
Every empire will perish!
And only law shall flourish!

Well then, let it flourish!
Let this Law flourish well!

Jihad[12]

They were destined for a wonderful future;
Adorned with brilliant intelligence,
They were the light of a nation,
The hope of a generation scattered, nourished,
By thoughts of evolution and revolution.

On the internet, they found a new cause,
A cause that turns cultures against cultures,
A cause that causes the clash of cultures,
A cause that is the source of community tensions,
Religious hatred, ideological conflicts, and identity
crises!

A cause that sparks the war of all against each,
The war of each against all!
A cause that opposes all diversity,
But a cause that promotes the uniformity of thought
In the city, among diverse entities and municipalities!

This cause that destroys critical thinking and glorifies
The spirit of criticism,
This cause that destroys world peace with
A mere flick of the wrist.
This cause that spoke to their hearts and emotions
Is none other than: extremism.

This doctrine had promised them mountains and
wonders,
A life of fighters for causes of awakening,
A life of struggle against unparalleled enemies!

---

[12] For a world of peace and openness.

37

A destiny of heroines and heroes feeling entrusted
with a mission
Unique to a very unique time.
A destiny that would forever engrave their names in
marble and on sacred trees,
A destiny that would elevate them to the pantheon of
political glory!

Yet the cause is far from being noble!
Young girls are reduced to slavery,
Forced to reproduce as in breeding farms.

Yet they must fight democracy by promoting
The rise of a world marked by fear,
A world in which each remains in their own,
A world where the only language is that of tanks,
A world that legitimizes the language of terror!

The internet is said to be the origin of this deviation;
Yet, the internet is supposed to ensure the progress
of humanity,
In diversity and in a harmony of conviviality!

Do we, then, have the right to turn the internet
Into a vehicle of hate sometimes leading to terror?
Do we, then, have the right to pit communities
Against individuals and individuals against
communities?
And communities against communities?

It is time to shift the emphasis
From our differences to celebrating together our
Different accents!

It is time to stop all confusion
And everything related to it!

It is time to stop weaponizing the word
Radicalization, which degenerates into various ills,
That could be avoided with simple words!

No to hatred against a community!
No to hatred against a spirituality!
No to hatred against a certain idea!

Doesn't the diversity of colors in a tapestry enhance
its beauty?

Planetary Village[13]

We do not belong to the generation of letters,
We do not belong to the past world
And its outdated devices,
Now classified in museums!
We do not belong to that generation!

We belong to the generation of emails,
The generation of spam and trash bins,
The digital generation and its devices!
The generation of iPads and iPhones,
The generation of iCloud and iPods!
The generation of Facebook, Twitter, WhatsApp,
The generation of Instagram and telegram.

Social networks destroy barriers,
They break down entire borders.
Social media brings landscapes closer,
Individuals, communities, countries,
And the world becomes a very large village!

It is possible for a Matlakala from Cape Town,
To communicate with an Okala from Fredericton;
It is now possible for a Sanchez from Lima,
To exchange with a Fernandez from Accra!

But it is difficult for a Kenfack from Foto,
To meet his cousin Tsafack from Foto.
But it is difficult for a Traoré from Bamako,
To meet his brother Konaré from Sikasso.

---

[13] For more humane social relations.

When we know they are from the same village!
When we know they share the same landscape!
When we know they come from the same swamp!
When we know they live in the same hamlet!

Social media plunges us
Into a fantastical world
That can sometimes be too fantastic,
To be purely truthful!

A world of appearance,
And the cult of appearance.
A world simply virtual
And far from being real,
With its calvaries, its spaces, and eras,
Bringing distant people closer,
And pushing close people away!

Privacy was once sacred,
Intimacy was sanctified and valued,
Good reputation was praised,
And the golden belt was condemned!

Under the empire of social networks,
Our generation has no more privacy,
Our generation has neither intimacy,
Nor good reputation, but perhaps
A golden belt!

New scourges growing like
Sea mushrooms,
While becoming sea serpents,
Have risen above the fray!

Cyberbullying, cyber-intimidation,
Cybercrime, cyber-prostitution,
Cyberterrorism, cyber-voyeurism!

Here lies the daily life of the Android generation,
Here are the ingredients of the android world!

Our generation suffers and chokes
From cyber-dependence,
A real social cancer that hinders its growth.
A real sea serpent that paralyzes
Its emergence!

Our generation is stifled by a lack of culture,
Which fosters the rise of uncultured mindsets,
Mindsets opposed to societal debate,
But which signal the breakthrough of ideological
And political extremism in various lands!

Let us not be manipulated
By social networks that divide
Communities when the world
More than ever needs to smoke
The peace pipe!

Let us not be manipulated
By social media that, in the face of social controversy,
Pour oil on the fire,
When the belligerents need
To tune their instruments,
In order to play music better!

What are these networks that hinder reading,

Writing, and the debate of ideas?
What are these networks that oppose the
Weight of ideas and the strength of arguments?
What are these media that restrict access
To quality information?
What are these networks that undermine harmony
While glorifying cacophony?

Where is the human in this world
Of techno-science?
Where is the real society in these social media?
Does human warmth have a price?
Is real reputation worth a golden belt?

Is virtual life always a reflection
Of real life?

They are Queens![14]

Women are lionesses ready to confront
This world of beasts that offers them not
The lion's share, from their gazelle-like stature.

Women are sacred queens,
Wearing colors of dignity,
Of proven magnanimity and hospitality!

They are the source of life and survival,
Sowing love between lovers, harmony,
Among belligerents at daggers drawn.

They have the power to move cities
Towards ascensions of prosperity,
Towards directions of intelligibility.
They are the becoming, the future of the community!
Curiously, some women still remain
Victims of domestic violence.
Even today, the role of women is reduced
To providing illegal effort,
Just as is asked of a donkey or a horse
In a less-than-ideal scenario!

She is still regarded
In many lands,
As a machine for production,
A machine for reproduction!

Quality education is a dream in some places,

---

[14] For the empowerment of women and the recognition of their sacred rights!

Female genital mutilation, a reality under other skies!
Reproduction in a healthcare context,
An illusion in many spheres,
The protection of her body, a mere chimera!

Women remain mere toys of history,
Passively witnessing the games and stakes of history!

Isolated from political power, anti-feminist,
She can only applaud macho laws.
Isolated from economic power, she is condemned
To remain a humiliated consumer,
In a world dominated by entrepreneurship,
A world dominated by patriarchy!

Poverty is sexist!
Poverty is sexist!

The woman, no matter her treasures!
She has the right to the respect of her body!
The right to the respect of her dignity!
The right to quality education!
The right to reproductive health!
The right to participate in ambitions!
The right to the power of production!
The right to non-discrimination,
Because she is a queen!

If they did not exist, they would have to be created,
So that they could reign!

How can one conceive of a world devoid of queens?
Such a world would be odorless, colorless!

Such a world would be bland and without rum or
aromas!

It is she who gives life!
It is she who knows the pains of pregnancy,
And various means of survival!
She is the first nurse,
She is our refuge, the nourishing breast!
She is also our best advisor!
Because she is a queen!

Why then so much hatred against women?
Why not uphold their sacred rights?
Why not give back to her beautifully,
At least part of what she has given us?

Because they are all queens!
They all have the capacity to change
This haunted world,
Its numerous flaws and avatars!

Can we allow women
To have access to quality education?
May we allow law and justice to prevail,
Flowing like an unquenchable river,
They are queens!

Let women's rights be respected!
Let women influence
Political life, the business world!
Civil society, the world of performing arts!
The judicial world, the world of science!
High finance, national defense!
Public safety, and diplomacy,

Because they are all queens!

In a fairer and more equitable world,
A world that empowers queens,
We can finally dare to dream of seeing
Ourselves illuminated through their luminous rays,
Like a beautiful sunbeam,
Like a firefly lighting the path
In the heart of the dark night.
They are queens!

They are born to illuminate the world,
With their rays, oh so bright,
With their shimmering colors,
With their emerging intelligence.

Yet, we must recognize their sacred right,
Yet, we must honor them!
Yet, we must sanctify them!
Yet, we must heroize them!
Yet, we must elevate them,
Above the fray!
Yet, we must magnify them!

The recognition of the value of women should
Happen now or never!
It will certainly require a sacrifice:
The revolution!
A revolution that has all its meaning, its
quintessence,
Its essence, and even its substance,
Because they are all queens!

And can embody the change
We would like to see blossom, like the dawn
In the world!

Women are amazons!
They are lionesses!

They are all queens!
And can change the world!

Glimmer of Hope!

March eighth reminds us of adversities,
For the triumph of equality,
A sacred struggle for great diversity,
In societies that are sometimes hierarchical!

A day of reflection,
On various inequalities
That persist in society!

A day that performs the autopsy
Of women's rights violations,
Victims of infamous discrimination.
A day that values women,
By recognizing their achievements!

A day of acknowledgment,
In the Great Renaissance,
Of the leadership that women
Play with a certain ease;
In communities,
And in many households
Across societies!

A day that calls upon us
To restore the image of women,
To give women back,
At least part of what they
Contribute without boasting,
In a world littered with zeal:

The zeal of marginalization,
The zeal of humiliation,

The zeal of intimidation,
The zeal of predation!

This is not a day of debacle,
Nor a day reserved for garments,
Not even a day of escalation,
Or a day without real propaganda!

This is not a day of folklore,
In the name of airy recognition,
Never fully engraved in marble,
Or a debate to simply close,
When legal protection struggles to blossom!

It is not a commercial day either,
That sacrifices feminist interests,
At the altar of corporate stakes;
Nor a day of pure ceremony,
Without real memorial content!

Yet it is a day of action,
A day of awareness,
A day of revolution,
A day of evolution,
A day of consciousness-raising.

For the rights of women to live,
For the rights of girls to live,
For female leadership to thrive!

Beyond the symbolism of March eighth,
Beyond the ceremonial aspects of March,
May such a day
Join the useful with the pleasant.

Ethics to aesthetics,
Legality to legitimacy,
Promotion to protection,
Of women's rights!

Rights recognized for women,
Simply because they are women!
Rights for which generations
Have sacrificed for other generations!

Only then could these beautiful ones emerge,
Who, like swallows,
Announce Spring.

This magical time
That celebrates the nectar of flowers
And exalts the fragrance of flowers,
From dawn to the last hour,
Eliciting the greatest joy,
Not just for a part of the people,
But for all the people,
Because it is fully legal!
Because it is entirely equal!

The Goat Grazes Where it is Tied![15]

The countries of the South are linked to their
imperial power,
Like by an umbilical cord!
This umbilical cord persists through conventions
That weigh on them like a sword of Damocles.
Leaders have not always secured the interests
Of the people for whom they committed!
They remain the invisible hand of scattered interests
That do not help the interests of the nation,
Because the goat grazes where it is tied!

Francophone states paid allegiance to Paris,
Anglophone states to London,
Lusophone states to Lisbon,
Hispanophone states to Madrid.

The governance of young nations is a disaster;
This governance that strays from the norm,
By normalizing the deviation, leads to a huge cancer,
Undermining public finances and public authorities,
Positioned as governors and public budget
administrators,
Positioned as scavengers and foxes of public wealth,
Because the goat grazes where it is tied!

Public fortune merging with private fortune,
Private fortune unjustly enriching itself from the
treasury,
The State becoming like a private enterprise,

---

[15] Contribution to fighting corruption and promoting good
governance!

Development aid becoming a blessing for the
privileged,
Administrative competitions, a real market,
Election deadlines, a real masquerade won
By the one who holds the strings of a fat purse,
The justice system. a true auction market,
State servants wealthier
Than entrepreneurs, bankers, or financiers,
Because the goat grazes where it is tied!

Because it is necessary to consolidate the power
received from
Paris, Madrid, London, or Lisbon,
And that the power exercised comes from abroad!

Because the State remains a cash cow
To be exploited to the bone,
Because it is necessary to grease the beard of the
godfather,
The political godfather, the sovereign godfather!

Because one must carve out a place in the sun,
And society values criminals
More than citizens with a republican conscience,
Because one becomes a cantonal elite
That must ensure, through unscrupulous maneuvers,
The victory of its faction in electoral deadlines,
Because the goat grazes where it is tied!

The public service is a national cake,
The public service is a regional feeding trough,
Elections are a way to access the trough,
Appointments are a distribution of the national cake.
The minister is a departmental minister

Yet, supposed to embody the national community,
Regardless of his tribal or local affiliation,
Because the goat grazes where it is tied!

Corruption remains a social cancer
That eats away at the very core
Of African states,
And many other South American states!

How will we make the South shine if
The bull is not seized by the horns?
How will we illuminate this world
If an internal revolution does not take place through
Governance and ethical approaches?

Africa must undergo an internal revolution
That would exorcise it of many ghosts:
The ghost of corruption;
The ghost of embezzlement;
The ghost of megalomania;
The ghost of kleptomania;
The ghost of financial crime;
The ghost of financial mismanagement.

Because here, the goat browses where it is tied,
But it is also in this place that it must be marked
And bitten by an adored serpent!

The serpent of the fight against corruption,
Which would make the South
A land of ethics in public affairs!

A land where milk and honey flow for all!

A land where drinking water flows for everyone!
A land where salt and bread are abundant!
Happiness, flourishing and sparkling for all!

Pan-African Dream[16]

Africa remains the cradle of humanity,
The cradle of advanced civilizations,
The nurturing breast of humanity,
Even if Africa remains balkanized,
Even if it continues to be humiliated!

It has suffered from the slave trade,
Which deprived it of a significant part
Of its population, of its human resources!

It has suffered from colonization,
Which turned the African into a sub-human, deprived
Of his culture and authenticity,
A sub-human deprived of his identity,
A man entirely apart,
Deprived of his oil, his gold, and his treasures!

It suffers from neo-colonialism
Due to its evolution in scattered ranks!

In Berlin, they divided the African continent like
vultures.
They divided African families,
They divided communities,
Divided African empires
That brought glory and pride
To the African people, adorned
With their magnified civilization!

Today, Africa remains a shadow of itself,

---

[16] For a united and prosperous Africa.

Africa remains the theater of supreme misery,
Africa remains a sacrificed land,
In which politicized conflicts proliferate,
Economically flavored wars,
Media-ethnic confrontations,
Pitting Africans against Africans!

Yet Africa has never been divided,
Africans are one glorified people.
Its current borders are opposed
To the spirit of unity, uniqueness, and solidarity,
That hovers over every African son and daughter,
Africanity stands against the borders imposed
By imperialism, now condemned!

Africa remains a toy of globalization,
Its voice is despised in the concert of nations.
Africa remains this incapable major, without
ambition,
An eternally tutored major, under guardianship
Of a so-called international community,
Crowned with highly liberal values,
Which, extraordinarily, is imperial!

Africa must unite,
Africans must unite.

Because Africans are one people,
Because the borders are mere facades,
Because Africa must speak with one voice
In a world of powerful voices!

Africa must unite, or else it risks perishing
And languishing on the periphery of globalization!

The unity of Africa will allow Africans
To move from Cape to Cairo,
From Dakar to Madagascar,
From Pretoria to Mombasa,
From Casablanca to Douala,
From Conakry to Djibouti!

The unity of Africa will lead to:
An African diplomacy that will defend its interests
In a world dominated by superpowers;
An African army that would limit the powers
Of foreign nations and their disconcerting agendas!
An agricultural policy for Africa!

That would keep famine and misery at bay;
An African currency that, with care,
Would grant sovereignty to the economy!

An African passport that would facilitate mobility
Across the continent and ensure respect for Africans
At the air, sea, and land borders of closed countries!

The unity of Africa will spare Africa
From community tensions because
An African finally becomes a brother to another
African,
Because Africa's diversity is a
Fuel for the African nation,
A nation with the colors of the rainbow,
Rich in its natural and perpetual cultural diversity,
To the sound of brotherly love!

How can we achieve this ideal if
National sovereignties persist,
If an African remains a stranger in Africa,
If the lack of will toward this peaceful ideal
Of African unity persists?

How can we achieve it
If there is still a difficult sovereignty?
If it is difficult for an African
To visit his own city
In great tranquility,
And if customs barriers remain valued?

Africa must gather her children,
To the rhythm of the famous Magnificat,
And around a wood fire
Sprinkled with raffia wine!

It must heal its childhood wounds,
And bruises, look at itself in a mirror,
Without breaking that mirror!

Africans must smoke the peace pipe,
A peace of hearts and not a peace of cemeteries,
A peace that would allow the sons and daughters
Of Africa, all beautiful and whole,
To tune their instruments to better play
The music!

A music that will emerge from the depths
Of its sacred forests, from its sanctified savannas,
A music with rhythms and dances
Of unity and brotherhood!

A music that, like the swallow,

Announces a new time under the sun,
The time of the Africa of wonders!

Africa will not perish like the Titanic
In the open sea!
Because it is a mother,
Loved by its mayors!
Loved by its peers!
And its hour of glory will ring when
It unites!

This glory will be like that of this
Pharaonic Africa,
This "Samory" Africa,[17]

This Africa of Sundiata Keita,
This Africa of Kankan Moussa,
This Africa of Shaka,
This Africa of the Soxhsa,
This Africa of Yennenga!

The wonderful Africa,
The glorious Africa,
The Africa of glories,
Glories at the curve
Of its empires of victories
And its famous histories!

Africa will awaken,
Africa will unite!
And when it unites,
The world will tremble!

---

[17] In reference to Samory Touré, hero of the Mali Empire.

Dirty Laundry is Washed at Home

When Europe sneezes,
Africans catch a cold.
When America sneezes,
Africa catches a cold.
And when Africa coughs,
It chokes, it chokes!

Africa suffers and chokes,
From problems in tufts;
Chronic economic crisis,
Almost chronic political crisis,
Cynical identity crisis!

Revolutionaries of Africa,
To oppose injustices,
Exert pressure on the West,
As if Africa were Eurafrica,
As if Africa were Afrimerica!

Foreign governments
Are called upon to share
Africa's problems,
Even though they are supposed to be foreign
To a continent that danced
Its independence to the beloved sound
Of a revolution so valued and adored!

Independence Cha Cha, this music
That made Africa vibrate with its hymns,
Celebrating physical and mystical battles
Against dramatic imperialism!

How can we understand that Africans
Can still believe that the Azanian salvation
Depends on the heartbeat
Of nations sometimes filled with resentment,
Against the nations of the African continent,
Against the African populations?

African political revolutions
Should be truly African.
Never will a phenomenon from other nations
Change the condition of the African man
Who must bring about his own change
From his own continent!

It is a dishonor to weaken one's nation
In front of other nations,
It is honorable to fight for one's nation
In one's homeland and with one's compatriots!

Let us remember that Africa will write
Its own history, and it will be,
From the north to the south of the Sahara,
A story of glory and dignity.[18]

Let us remember that in the concert
Of nations, there are no friends,
There are no enemies,
But there are only interests!

That the impoverishment of his nation
Will never make the African
A respected man in other nations

---

[18] See the last letter of Lumumba to his wife Pauline!

Where the law of the lions reigns supreme,
And in many cases, the law of retaliation!

No nation is exempt from problems.
The nation is like a family,
And in a family, when there is a problem,
It is resolved within the familial intimacy!

What good is it to hold European marches,
Or American meetings and settings,
In the face of African difficulties?
The peoples of Africa should
Gather around the African campfire,
To smoke the peace pipe,
And walk hand in hand,
Regardless of their differences,
Regardless of their divergences!

Isn't dirty laundry washed in the family?
Let's stop tarnishing the image of the African family
Before other Western families
That sometimes struggle
To solve their own family problems!

Africa is independent,
And cannot be dependent
Like this incapable finger
In international relations,
Under the boot and guardianship
Of other independent nations!

To think that the solution to Africa's problems
Lies in European or American space
Is like waiting for a boat at the airport,

In fact, waiting for a plane at the port,
Or thinking that a lion can dignify keep a sheepfold!

Can a lion really guard a sheepfold?

Banana Republic [19]

Vox populi, vox Dei,
The voice of the people, the voice of God!
Institutions would descend from the heavens,
And Power would come from the gods!

The western wind shook the coconut trees,
It overturned the safoutier trees,
It brought down the guava trees!
It shook over there,
The most imposing Baobabs!

From its ashes, democracy was born,
Which pronounces the funeral rites
Of political aristocracy,
Glorified by single parties and
Quasi-monarchic institutions!

The President of the Republic remains
Omnipotent and omnipresent,
The President of the Republic remains
All-powerful and hyper-influential.

He is the keystone of the system and
The strong man of the strong regime,
When the nascent republic has
Dedicated itself to consolidating
Strong institutions,
Controlled by other institutions!

The Parliament remains a box

---

[19] For the construction of strong institutions!

For recording presidential wills
And ministerial wishes!

The presidency controls the internal kitchen
Of the parliamentary chambers,
Its heartbeat, its blood pressure,
And even its love affairs!

The bills pass like a
Letter in the mail,
The parliamentary debate becoming a true
National theater,
Within the sacred institution
Of the bicameral parliament!

Who simulates the practice of democracy.
Yet, the democratic ideal
Would have the parliament independently control
The actions of the executive power,
And its administrative variants!

The judiciary is nonexistent
As a national institutional entity!
The President of the Republic remains the
Attorney General of the nation!

It is he who decides the appropriateness
Of prosecutions.
It is still he who appoints and revokes
The judges and their staff!
It is always he who decides the status
Of the judiciary!

He is the alpha and the omega of national justice,

Which remains hidden in the shadows,
Acting through an invisible hand,
An iron fist in a velvet glove,
Like a wolf disguised as a lamb.

The magistrate is a loyal dignitary
To the imperial party,
Or to the party close to the imperial party!

He has made sacrifices at the watering hole
To benefit from the graces of the great Manitou,
He must remain faithful to the ideals of the party,
In order to avoid falling into disgrace
And being thrown into the dustbin of history!

Isn't justice supposed to demonstrate
Independence?
Shouldn't the judiciary
Neutralize the executive within the framework
Of a free and democratic society?

The cult of personality
Is a favorite sport,
The sacralization, the heroization
And the sanctification of political power,
A valued practice!
The praises and songs in glory
Of the providential and eternal man,
A venerated practice!

The public thing is confused with the thing
Of the politician
Who, sitting at the trough, lives
In an insolent opulence,

In the heart of an ocean of misery.

When the Constitution limits mandates,
Political maneuvering takes place in the hinterland,
To provoke a revision of the constitution,
Which would be anti-democratic,
By preventing a candidate who
Still enjoys the trust of the people
From continuing his adventures at the top of
The State.
It's a real institutional theater
That breaks the foundations of democracy.

What is the fate of the rule of law
In this Hollywood scenario?
Shouldn't power stop power?
What is civil society doing?
And where are the opponents?
What are they doing?

Our republics remain
Tyrannical and despotic regimes,
Masked with colors and democratic façades!
Our republics remain
Under the influence of strongmen,
When we need strong institutions!

Our republics must adorn themselves
With colors as bright
As they are sparkling,
With a vibrant rule of law,
And a living democracy!

Tropical Opponent[20]

Power is not power
Without the presence of counter-powers!
Counter-powers should,
In a free and democratic society,
Neutralize and stop the power,
In a democratic spirit!

Yet, counter-powers must
Be held by dignified
And noble men who embody the ethics of power!
Moreover, the political opponent
Must genuinely be an opponent,
Who practices political opposition
And not political juxtaposition,
Which even makes the opponent an unacknowledged
ally
Of the system, of the political regime,
Established in perpetual and supreme governance!

Being an opponent means criticizing the power
To improve its action, or,
To tenaciously conquer said power!

Being an opposition figure is not just about criticizing
For the sake of criticizing,
It's not about staying close to power
To feed off the popular soup,
Or contesting power by day
And happily marrying that same power by night!

---

[20] For a Republican Opposition!

Being in opposition means performing wonders,
Being capable of going
To the ultimate sacrifice to make
Triumph the cause for which one dedicates
Their political existence!

In the tropics, the opposition figure remains
A political entrepreneur who, like an operator,
Sacrifices the people at the twenty-third hour
For their first-hour interests!
They are a politician who, at dawn, stirs the nation,
Arousing its emotions against the governing order,
But at dusk, dines with the same rulers!

They are an opportunist, a political careerist,
A self-centered individual, a beggar for troughs,
Disguised as a political opponent!

In Parliament, they openly denounce
The authoritarian tendencies of the government,
But bend their backs to receive
Financial favors from the government.
In Parliament, they support the government
In its anti-democratic tendencies,
As long as their paycheck
Is secured, their benefits consolidated!

Under the tropics, the opposition is nonexistent,
But persistent juxtaposition!
The opponents have no political conviction,
Politics being a means to carve out a place
In the sun, at the expense of the sovereign people
Martyred, tested, and impoverished,

By submarine politicians!

In the tropics, the opponent is not
An opponent defending the interests of a part
Of the people for a time, or all the time!
They are merely an agitator in political life
Who becomes virulent when
Deprived of the purse strings!

How are we going to build
Strong institutions
If the opposition does not constitute the condiment
Of democracy?

If the opposition does not constitute the cement
Of democracy?
If the opposition is the refuge of political delinquents!

What are these opponents without political
conviction
Who do not control government action,
For private interests?
Who violate the will of the sovereign people,
And pose as occult accomplices of
Kleptocracy, oligarchy, and the prevailing
gerontocracy?

What are these opponents?
Who juxtapose themselves with the dominant party
When it's time to oppose?
What are these opponents,
Who warehouse and superimpose
On the predominant and superpower party?

What are these opponents,
Who do not know what it means to oppose?

They have forgotten that politics is a priesthood!
That politics is above all a commitment,
A priestly commitment!
That politics is nothing but a priesthood!
And nothing but a priesthood!

That the politician is a man of principle,
And of convictions who holds to his principles,
A noble man ready to sacrifice himself
For the social cause that is dear to him!

They have forgotten that the opposition
Is not a matter of position,
That the opposition is not a matter of positioning,
That the opposition is not a matter of taking a stance!
That the opposition is not juxtaposition,
And that juxtaposition is a matter of position,
Which durably paralyzes the action of the opposition!

They have forgotten that the politician
Is not an economic operator!
And that in his role as a political opponent,
He has a historical responsibility!
Because he is invested with a particular mission,
At a very particular moment,
And in a very particular era,
They have forgotten!

Light of the World[21]

Youth is the hope of the world,
It is they who can revolutionize the world
Through innovative approaches,
Through emerging social engagement.
Youth is the future of the world,
When it discovers its mission,
When it fulfills such a mission.

Some young people are still spectators
Of social and economic life!
Some young people still remain observers
Of the spheres of political power!
Some young people are still waiting for everything
from the State,
Yet the State does not necessarily know
Their condition!

Young people have deserted libraries,
To take refuge in media centers,
To linger in nightclubs!

Youth no longer rise, no longer dream,
Because a certain gerontocracy
Assassinates their certain dreams.

It is not, however, a well-kept secret,
Youth is beautiful,
And with zeal, constitutes the potential
Of societies that make room for it.

---

[21] For Youth!

73

Some young people have improved the scientific
world!
Some young people have revolutionized politics!
Some young people have disrupted the
Economic, physical, and technological arenas!

It was young people who dreamed
And firmly believed in a happy future!
It was young people who read
And knew that the future would shine brightly!
It was young people who were unafraid!
Unafraid of adventures and misadventures!
They were not afraid of the known and the unknown!
Unafraid of the most ridiculous humiliations!

Youth is the salt of the Earth,
Youth is the queen of eras,
Youth, with its zeal and wings,
Should go forth to conquer the skies:
Young people are the light of the world!

This light that, in the dark night,
Illuminates the world like a streetlight,
In the air and in the nocturnal depths.

Young people are lamps
That must dream and conquer
Nations.

Young people are lights
That cannot be extinguished,
That must illuminate societies.
They must not be afraid,
Even in the face of misfortune!

They should have the audacity to hope,
Even when the direction of the wind
Blows against their right to hope!

Because young people are the salt of the Earth,
Because young people are the light of the world,
Because young people are the hope of nations!

Like the goose that lays golden eggs,
Youth should be glorified!
Young people should be cherished!
Youth should be nurtured!

They are the salt of the Earth!
They are the light of the world!

Lagoon Ebrié[22]

In the air rose the beauty
Of a city in its wisdom.
In the air, the supremacy
Of strong ports and sought-after airports:

Abidjan, the city of the most beautiful,
Abidjan, the lovely gazelle-like;
Abidjan, the entity of sun rays;
Abidjan, the mega city with a taste of honey.

Cradled by the Atlantic Ocean,
The locality is one of the most peaceful.
Elevated by its magnificent values,
The land inspires a vision of Africa,
And its trends, oh, how idyllic

Adorned with a dynamic youth
That rises from its energetic actions,
Equipped with a youth of activist demeanor
Ready, with its flaming dynamism,
To inject the new dynamic
That makes this philanthropic city
An oasis of prosperity under the tropics.

In Abidjan, the youth are entrepreneurs
And are building an Africa free from fears.
The youth here act in the early hours,
To avoid the twenty-third hour.
Their achievements will bring happiness

---

[22] An Adventure in Abidjan.

To all those still trapped in misfortune.

Abidjan is also the joy of living,
Even when some remain intoxicated.
Abidjan is the vibe of people
Who have no choice but to live
In difficult places,
And in a blend of conviviality.

Abidjan is the coupé-décalé!
In wisdom!
It's slam in the city!
It's lyrical poetry,
In acoustic spaces!

It's a certain idea of Francophonie,
Working in harmony with the symphony,
Local linguistic authenticity!
It's a certain way of speaking French!

It's a taming of the French language,
A love for the French language,
Which, with humor, lives in happy coexistence,
And weds joyfully
With Ivorian traditions,
African traditions!
Rooted in the history of Côte d'Ivoire;
The history of its ivory towers;
The history of its luminous kingdoms!
Which brings glory to the Ébrié lagoon!

Abidjan is not a city of owls!
Abidjan is not an island of marabouts!
Abidjan is the sweetest!
Abidjan is the sweetest in the world!

Ouidah[23]

We had come, driven
By a high spirit of curiosity;
We had come with the hope
Of understanding the twists of history!

The deep history of Africa;
The history of Africa's lions;
And not that of the hunters!
The sad history of slavery;
The dark history of severance,
Which separated from Mother Africa,
Her children, in a tragic climate!

Ouidah, land of the Agoudah!
It was right here that Black people
Paid a heavy price for being Black;
It was right here that Black people
Were tortured and martyred;
Kings humiliated;
Civilizations overthrown;
Notables tortured;
Great sages captured;
By zealous predators!

It was right here that the African Man
Was sold as a commodity;
It was right here that he had to renounce
Against his will, his thoughts, his ideas,
To serve a master without faith or law,
Who does not respect human rights,

---

[23] An Adventure in Cotonou.

Simply because they are human!

With emotion, we have seen;
With our own eyes, we have seen
The remnants of the slave trade,
The museum of the slave trade;
The route taken by the slavers;
This road of no return;
Which tore thousands of Africans
From their sacred land, the land of Africa!

Filled with emotion, we have seen;
The tree of forgetfulness that consecrated
The cultural alienation of the African,
To the detriment of American visions!
Of European visions!

We have seen, with our own eyes
The tree of return;
Which promised the African a return
To his land, only in spirit;
We have seen the door of no return;
Which tore the African from his homeland,
With no other hope
Of ever finding his territory again!

The slave trade was a crime against
The Black People, a crime against
Humanity in its various regions,
A crime whose true acknowledgment
Remains in the shadows;
But above all, remains hidden in the dark!

The current world, supposedly evolved,

Gives the impression that this morose past
Is not always past!
And that the injustice is not already enough!

May justice remain inexhaustible,
And finally flow like an unending torrent!
May the world repair
This immeasurable harm!

Let justice, all justice!
And nothing but justice, illuminate
This world of precipices,
And its multiple torments!

Bucharest[24]

We dreamed of a better world,
We had all come from elsewhere,
Fueled by a revolutionary spirit,
And a voluntary approach!

Bucharest, a bird's eye view from Everest,
It was here that the engaged youth
Of the world displayed their fierceness,
Against the injustices that oppress
Our societies, at the antipodes of tenderness!

We came from Romania!
We came from Armenia!
We came from Italy!
We came from the Americas!
We came from Europe!
We came from Africa!

We shared the ideal of a just world!
We were a family united by justice!
We wanted justice to be the same,
And for the rule of law to no longer be a problem!
We believed in the strength of civil society,
And its beneficial actions in the cities!

We discussed with vitality,
And in a climate of conviviality!
We witnessed the birth of this brotherhood,
Around this struggle for freedom!
We were but a community,

---

[24] Memory of an Adventure in Romania and Eastern Europe.

Despite our great diversity!

Bucharest gives rise to a youth,
Determined to combat the laziness
That allows various pettiness to persist!
International civil society and its youth
Can influence the course of a world
That respects rights and freedoms!

A world exorcised of racism!
A world exorcised of anti-Semitism!
A world anesthetized from machismo!
A world anesthetized from denialism!
A world that respects its diversity!
A world that respects equality!
A world that condemns hate crimes!
A world that says no to hate!

Bucharest, this meeting place of judicial flavors!
Bucharest, this city of revolutionary scents!
Oh! Bucharest, for your spirit of enlightenment,
And your sparks blooming with forgiveness,
Bucharest, we love you!

The Sun Shines in the West[25]

The sun was setting with zest,
As night already fell in the East,
The fireflies illuminated our
Nocturnal paths with generosity.
And we moved forward with boldness,
In search of a flame of hope,
Nestled in the moon, the stars, or the sun!

The East was drowned in fog,
The East was plunged into a dark night.
Only in the West did the sun appear;
Since the first cockcrow, the sun
Rose with awakening colors,
While in the West, it shone with its rays
Sprinkled with glimmers of expectation!

Winnipeg and its historical museums,
A particularly atypical city,
Scattered by the very mythical Red River,
Around which historical battles
For the Manitobans and their linguistic rights
Were fought on the shores of red lakes,
Stained with the blood of historical defenders.

Winnipeg, affectionately known as Winterpeg
For its winter with Siberian accents,
The hospitality of its authentic populations,
Despite a rather very wintry winter.
A summer with Sahelian accents,
Despite the freshness of its exotic flora!

---

[25] Memory of an Adventure in the Prairies and the Pacific!

83

In the heights of the Museum of Human Rights,
The roofs of Saint Boniface rise,
Along with its glorious edifices.
In the splendor of this tower of hope,
St. Boniface University stands out,
The historic St. Boniface Cathedral,
The historic St. Boniface Museum,
The burial site of the emblematic Louis Riel,
The very imposing Louis Riel College,
This jewel of Manitoba's Francophonie!
Winnipeg is a hub of performing arts,
And its very famous patrons!
Winnipeg also offers enchanted evenings
In the nooks of the Cercle Molière Theatre,
And its well-renowned actors,
Who embody the local culture with mastery!

How can one not remember
The Festival du Voyageur, with its widely
Artistic and cultural colors!
How can one not remember
The improvised evenings and the joy
Of witnessing spectacular and diverse actors?

How can one not remember?
Those heated discussions with Konaré,
Dressed in his white gandoura,
Reminding us of a forgotten Africa,
In the heart of the prairies, yet so celebrated?

How can one not remember
Those prestigious conversations with Manené,
The symbol of a well-integrated Quebecer

In the distant lands of the prairies?

Because the sun shines here!

Saskatoon, in the heart of Saskatchewan,
Regina, a stone's throw from Alberta,
We couldn't resist the magnificence
Of the vast prairie and its depths,
Its stretches of verdant lands,
Upon which roamed majestic cattle
Feeding on their lush green meals!

Jasper, the land of hopeful souls,
We couldn't resist the beauty
Of this land that generously gives
Wonderful reasons to keep hoping!

We couldn't resist the diversity
Of its beautiful and cherished people,
We couldn't help but be swept away
By its sacred hills,
Its architecture of timeless charm,
And its tradition of great hospitality.

Because the sun shines here!

Vancouver, the beautiful city of the Pacific,
Or "Hongcouver" for its Asian values;
We couldn't resist its sunsets,
Which, like its sunrises,
Give the taste of life far from the Atlantic!

Bordered by iconic and enchanting beaches

That evoke the tales of Alice in Wonderland,
And with beautiful and marvelous architecture,
Vancouver is the economic gem
Of the brilliant and flourishing British Columbia!

In Vancouver, nature remains generous,
Its mountains highly majestic,
Opportunities ever flourishing,
The future inevitably dazzling.

Because the sun shines here!

The dazzling Victoria, seat of political power
In charming British Columbia,
Haloed by its history, oh, so sanctified,
Its people steeped in great serenity,
And its beaches sumptuously bathed in sunlight!

Victoria, it's the University of Victoria,
With its vast knowledge and partnerships,
In a world of volunteerism,
Built far from patriarchy!

It's letting yourself be carried away,
By the flora, the waves of the Pacific Ocean,
It's savoring Pacific salmon,
In an atmosphere most enchanting!

It's living in peace,
It's sharing peace,
It's smoking the peace pipe!

It's having the courage to hope,
It's always hoping,

It's always having reasons to prosper!

Because the sun shines here!

It's finally seeing the sun rise,
It's watching it set,
It's always seeing the sun rise,
It's watching it shine and sparkle,
To find reasons to exist,
To find reasons to hope,
In majestic conviviality!

Savoring the delights of its days,
The delights of the most beautiful of our days,

Because the sun shines here!

Postface

The Author

A jurist trained at the University of Ottawa, Montreal, and Moncton, André Blondel Tonleu Mendou is widely recognized for his many distinctions throughout his academic and professional journey. He was Vice-World Champion of French-speaking debate at the University of Paris-Sorbonne, recipient of the SAÉ scholarship at the University of Montreal, laureate of the Africa 35.35 Youth Awards in the Advocacy and Civil Society category, listed among the top 35 most influential young Francophones, and included in the top 100 most positively influential young Africans. He was also a distinguished advocate in the International Moot Court Competition at the Faculty of Law at the University of Pretoria.

Despite these accolades that highlight his oratory skills, André Blondel is far from being just a speaker; he is also a man of action and a staunch humanist. This led him, in 2018, to join UN-HCR as an ambassador within the New World Institute to promote and defend the rights and cause of refugees and displaced persons. He has also mentored young students in various advocacy competitions to promote French-speaking oral culture at the University of Victoria and as a Francophone ambassador within the Saanich/Victoria School District in British Columbia.

In this work, he adopts a revolutionary stance advocating for the self-determination of African peoples, particularly of Black individuals, with his acute sense of freedom, fraternity, and equality among all humans; this collection of poems is neither political nor separatist. It emerges from a unique and well-crafted poetic style whose foundations lie in a desire for unity and equitable justice among all people of the world.

The Work

Versets du Pacifique is a collection of poems through which the author addresses Africans, the West, and most importantly, expresses his perspective on Black people worldwide. Through this collection, he invites readers to become aware of the condition of Black men and women in a world that has increasingly become racist, segregationist, tribalist, clannish, and chauvinistic.

This issue is undoubtedly a key reason that motivated the author to write this collection, *Versets du Pacifique*, which seems to take a different path and style from that of the earlier African poets, addressing the disenfranchised across the globe, regardless of their skin color, religious beliefs, or political convictions.

Thus, in *Versets du Pacifique*, the author challenges Western ideologies about Black people and the African continent, much like the early poets of the Négritude movement: Aimé Césaire, Léopold Sédar Senghor, to name just a few, with whom the author proudly identifies.

In this collection, the poet is wholly committed to the fight for a free and open world, a world governed by a system of elevated values that form the foundation of every well-organized society or people, values that make human life so precious it deserves to be protected: liberty, fraternity, equality, dignity, justice, and rights.

Peace, freedom of expression, and the right to protest, among other themes, are deeply present in this collection of poems.

It is also through these poetic verses that the author appears to criticize the West for confining its civilizing mission to a system of adaptation for others, presenting itself as the sole model, while disregarding the socio-cultural, economic, political, and environmental alienations, the power dynamics, and the systems of oppression that affect the entire Black society and Africa in particular, which is nonetheless "the cradle of humanity, the cradle of civilizations, the cradle of nations."

"The Black man faces a system,
Skillfully established, like a real problem,
And like a stone in his shoe,
Blocks his integration into the system!"

Demba Seck, PhD
Sociologist
dseck81@gmail.com

Acknowledgments

To Demba Seck, Sylvie Bollini, Yemene Jean, Geneviève Richer, Moïse Mougnan, Sydi Mohamed Cissé, Claude Gilles Djoumessi, Évariste Manéné, Amanda Carrasco, Mary An Laceste, Nadine Yanmo.

And to:

Ariane Mendou, Euloge Pascale Mendou, Sorel Mendou, Chrysologue Mendou, and Boniface Cellini Mendou Zeubou.

Previously Published by Éditions Grenier

NOVELS

- Annick Diop, *Profound Gaze*, 2009
- Marie Soeurette Mathieu, *A Step Towards the Matrix*, 2009
- Gladys Otou, *From One Ocean to Another*, 2008

NARRATIVE

- Léon Ouaknine, *Neither Here Nor There: Quebec, the Jews, and Me*, 2013
- Edgar Gousse, *The Bossale Republic: Alexis and the Carnivores of Power*, 2010

ESSAYS

- Stéphanie and Léon Ouaknine, *There Are No Subscribers to the Number You Called!*, 2009
- Bakary N'Badiallah Diarra, *Governance and Environment*, 2007
- Adrian Toumbi, *The Impact of September 11 on International Relations*, 2006
- Adrian Toumbi, *What Role for Nuclear Weapons in the 21st Century*, 2010
- Adrian Toumbi, *Powers and Strategies in Post-Cold War Europe*, 2021
- Herman J. Cohen, *Memoirs of a Diplomat*, 2018
- Mahamat Ali Youssouf, *Qatar's Quest for Aerospace*, 2016

POETRY

- Guy V. Amou, *The Roots of the Bonkul Dream of Silence*, 2010
- Yves Alavo, *Sublime Vertigos and Colors of Intimate Seasons*, 2010
- Frantz Mars, *Poetic Offering*, 2010
- Louisa M. En. Lafable, *Sea Effects or The Imprints of the Soul – 1st and 2nd Editions*, 2009
- Michel Sanon, *Kout Lanbi*, 2006
- Lhacène Ziani, *Tijeǧǧigin n Wawal*, 2005
- Fayez El Khoury, *A Creamy Sweetness (Digital Version)*, 2012

SOCIETY

- Nebardoum Derlemari, *The Mailloux Affair or the Confrontation with the Black Cause*, 2008
- Nebardoum Derlemari, *Quebec: A Hypocritical Society or the Misery of Immigration*, 2007
- Roger Taillibert, *Olympic Stadium of Montreal: Myths and Scandals*, 2010 (co-published with the French publishing house DILECTA)
- Yona Likongo, *Letter to My Children*, 2014

THEATER

- Guy V. Amou, *I Am Not an Exile*, 2017

THEOLOGY

- Enrico Joseph, *Would God Be Violent?*, 2005

THE GREAT INTERVIEWS

- Exclusive Interview with Kofi Annan, 2006

YOUTH

- Tanohé Ludovic N'Doly (screenplay) and Patrick Gopre (illustrations), *The Oath of Friendship*, 2021

SHORT STORIES

- Arnaud Segla, *The Point*, 2011